Success Tweets

For Finding a Job and Excelling in It

BILLIE SUCHER

&

BUD BILANICH

The Common Sense Guy

FRONT ROW PRESS

Front Row Press
191 University Boulevard, #414 • Denver, CO 80206 • 303.393.0446

This book is for our families:
Richard II, Sarah, Trey, Tessa Sucher
and Cathy Bilanich

xoxoxoxoxoxoxoxoxoxoxoxoxoxoxoxoxoxoxoxoxoxo
xoxoxoxoxoxoxoxoxoxoxoxoxoxoxoxoxoxoxoxoxoxoxo
xoxoxoxoxoxoxoxoxoxoxoxoxoxoxoxoxoxoxoxoxoxoxo
xoxoxoxoxoxoxoxoxoxoxoxoxoxoxoxoxoxoxoxoxoxoxo
xoxoxoxoxoxoxoxoxoxoxoxoxoxoxoxoxoxoxoxoxoxoxo
xoxoxoxoxoxoxoxoxoxoxoxoxoxoxoxoxoxoxoxoxoxoxo
xoxoxoxoxoxoxoxoxoxoxoxoxoxoxoxoxoxoxoxoxoxoxo

That's 140 hugs and kisses…

Thanks for your love and support.

Introduction

This is a career success book, done as 140 tweets. It will help you create the successful life and career you want and deserve.

It gives you 140 pieces of common sense career and life success advice, all in 140 characters or less.

It shows you how to find a job and excel in it, one tweet at a time. You'll get the essentials with no fluff.

Creating the life and career success you deserve should be fun and exciting. This book will show you what to do and how to do it.

Your time is valuable. You don't want to waste it. That's why you get 140 pieces of advice Twitter style, in 140 characters or less.

Building a successful career is simple common sense. It's not hard, but you need to do it right.

In this book, Billie Sucher will explain exactly what you need to do to find a job.

Bud Bilanich will explain what to do to excel in your job once you find it.

Billie focuses on career transitions, resume writing/personal branding, interviews, job search/networking, choices and motivation.

Bud focuses on personal responsibility, self confidence, positive personal impact, dynamic communication and relationship building.

The tweets that follow will show you how to create the life and career success you want and deserve.

Will tweet books replace traditional books? Probably not. But this little book will get you started creating a successful life and career.

Enjoy this book. But remember, we want to talk with you, not to you. Please follow us on Twitter @BillieSucher and @BudBilanich.

Please tweet about your thoughts on our ideas.

Each of the points we've made above is less than 140 characters.

See? You can communicate a lot of useful information in 140 characters or less. Enjoy these tweets.

Career
Transitions

CAREER TRANSITIONS

1

Yesterday is behind you; there is no better time than today to start over and create a new script for the tomorrow of your life.

CAREER TRANSITIONS

2

The first place to start when you lose your job is with the ending; celebrate 'what was' and take with you the best; let go of the rest!

CAREER TRANSITIONS

3

These three things: integrity, mastery and professionalism will make you stand out in a sea of competition.

CAREER TRANSITIONS

4

Before you decide what you want to do, consider these three basics: 1. passions 2. interests 3. abilities. Then identify desired options.

CAREER TRANSITIONS

5

Build a strong and vibrant transition team, truly invested in your sustained career success. Think: team sport versus solo expedition.

Résumé Writing/ Personal Branding

RÉSUMÉ WRITING / PERSONAL BRANDING

6

Do not ask "is my résumé good?" — ask, "Is my résumé effective in generating interviews?"

RÉSUMÉ WRITING / PERSONAL BRANDING

7

An effective résumé delivers the 'who, what and why' about a candidate before the reader can count to ten ... will yours?

RÉSUMÉ WRITING / PERSONAL BRANDING

8

Keep résumé content relevant, essential and supportive of your target goal.

RÉSUMÉ WRITING / PERSONAL BRANDING

9

Build your résumé to meet the specific needs of the job qualifications; to do otherwise will diminish the strength of your candidacy.

RÉSUMÉ WRITING / PERSONAL BRANDING

10

Before you begin to write a résumé, conduct self-analysis to discover your strengths, weaknesses and realistic value to the employer.

RÉSUMÉ WRITING / PERSONAL BRANDING

11

An effective résumé can be thought of as an enticing appetizer, awaiting the delectable entrée (Brand You) to follow thereafter.

RÉSUMÉ WRITING / PERSONAL BRANDING

12

View your professional résumé through the eyes of the employer; have you proven without question why you are worthy of an interview?

13

Integrate six key elements into your résumé: 1. Contact info 2. Goal 3. Profile 4. Experience 5. Education 6. Endorsements.

RÉSUMÉ WRITING / PERSONAL BRANDING

14

Add your LinkedIn URL and Twitter ID to your résumé once you have established several connections, recommendations and followers.

RÉSUMÉ WRITING / PERSONAL BRANDING

15

One error in your résumé can lead to your disqualification. Have three to five people proofread your résumé for mistakes and omissions.

RÉSUMÉ WRITING / PERSONAL BRANDING

16

Does your résumé adhere to this 6 C's of communication: clear, concise, consistent, credible, compelling, and a convincing call-to-action?

RÉSUMÉ WRITING / PERSONAL BRANDING

17

Review 10 examples of résumés on the Internet. If yours looks like "all the rest," start over so you will stand out and not blend in.

RÉSUMÉ WRITING / PERSONAL BRANDING

18

When using endorsements in your professional résumé, invite connections to write recommendations that support your job target.

RÉSUMÉ WRITING / PERSONAL BRANDING

19

Create ample white space in your résumé to project a sense of openness and an invitation to linger longer in digesting your unique story.

RÉSUMÉ WRITING / PERSONAL BRANDING

20

The thing about a résumé is that if you, the job seeker, don't love (or at least like) it, imagine the reader's response?

RÉSUMÉ WRITING / PERSONAL BRANDING

21

The best résumé ever written is of little value if the owner doesn't get it in the hands of hiring managers and decision makers.

RÉSUMÉ WRITING / PERSONAL BRANDING

22

Once your résumé is done, ask yourself: "Does my résumé sound like me?" The paper version and the in-person version will want to match up!

Interviews

INTERVIEWS

23

Leave no detail undone when preparing for your job interview. Make it effortless for the employer to 'get' the essence of Brand You.

INTERVIEWS

24

A confident smile, a firm handshake and
an upbeat, engaging conversation creates
a lasting first impression and a possible
job offer!

INTERVIEWS

25

Make it easy for the hiring team to learn how your credentials are a good match with their requirements. Prepare well and practice often.

26

Master the art of talking about y-o-u prior to speaking with employers, recruiters or networking contacts — a task well worth your time.

INTERVIEWS

27

By asking good questions, you will gain better data from which to draw conclusions about a particular job opportunity.

INTERVIEWS

28

Communicate with excellence about yourself and your brand, be it in your résumé, interview, emails, voice mails, texts or tweets.

INTERVIEWS

29

Strike the word 'interview' from your mind and replace it with 'business meeting,' a better known and more comfortable activity.

30

When rehearsing for an interview, consider 'sharing information' versus 'selling yourself' to enlighten listeners of your many merits.

INTERVIEWS

31

An interview is a chance to determine if you and the employer have anything in common. You won't know until you meet and learn more.

INTERVIEWS

32

You may be asked 'illegal' and/or 'inappropriate' interview questions. Respond to either with professionalism, calmness and confidence.

INTERVIEWS

33

Become an interesting conversationalist with people you know. Then, when you meet a stranger, it may be easier to strike up a conversation.

INTERVIEWS

34

Avoid distractions during the interview. Do not talk on your cell phone, text, or tweet. Be fully present and engaged with the hiring team.

INTERVIEWS

35

Prepare well for an interview and enter into the process with purpose, intention and a specific idea of the points you wish to convey.

INTERVIEWS

36

Mind your manners; say please, thank you and how may I help you? Not only is it polite and courteous, it will distinguish you.

INTERVIEWS

37

What is the one single thing that you have to offer that your competition doesn't? Know with certainty what it is before you interview.

INTERVIEWS

38

Just because you once made X amount of money doesn't mean that you will be entitled to that dollar figure now. Be willing to negotiate.

INTERVIEWS

39

Negotiate the best compensation package possible once a job offer is made. Until such time, you hold zero negotiation power.

Job Search/ Networking

JOB SEARCH / NETWORKING

40

Always protect your character and uphold the highest principles in your interactions with others.

JOB SEARCH / NETWORKING

41

Perseverance and consistency, necessary ingredients for today's job hunt. Both will propel you forward in your darkest days.

JOB SEARCH / NETWORKING

42

To find the courage to look for work when others say 'there are no jobs' may be the one single separator between you and your competition.

43

Before you go to an interview, put yourself in the hiring manager's seat. What expectations might you have of the candidate?

JOB SEARCH / NETWORKING

44

Looking for a new job requires a dogged determination, regardless of how tired, frustrated or demoralized you feel.

JOB SEARCH / NETWORKING

45

Consider finding new employment a privilege and doing a great job while you're at it, a responsibility.

JOB SEARCH / NETWORKING

46

Integrating creativity and ingenuity into your job hunt will distinguish you from your competition. Think: brand distinction.

JOB SEARCH / NETWORKING

47

View yourself as a product for sale in a highly saturated market. How will your credentials deliver more value and benefit to the employer?

JOB SEARCH / NETWORKING

48

Your attitude will make or break your job search. The best credentials in the world will not outshine a bad attitude.

JOB SEARCH / NETWORKING

49

Embrace the career transition process as an exciting new adventure with you as the project manager and dedicated driver behind everything!

JOB SEARCH / NETWORKING

50

Know yourself. Know what your brand stands for. Know what distinguishes you from your competition. Know why an employer 'should' hire you.

51

Identify the type of position you want and go after it with relentless fervor. Do not be deterred by events, elements, or the economy.

JOB SEARCH / NETWORKING

52

Take a direct route to getting hired and go straight to the source — the person who has the power and the authority to hire you.

JOB SEARCH / NETWORKING

53

Think unlike your competition is thinking; try every creative strategy, tactic, or idea imaginable to generate interviews.

54

You don't have to love looking for new employment; you just need to like it long enough to land a job offer!

JOB SEARCH / NETWORKING

55

The job market today is tough, competitive and even cruel. Do not stop looking for work. Never give up on yourself — or the search!

JOB SEARCH / NETWORKING

56

Be wary of turning your job search over to someone else. Always stay in the driver's seat to derive the most profitable results.

Choices

CHOICES

57

Before you decide not to go back to school to get that certificate or finish the degree, ask yourself, why not?

CHOICES

58

Who is holding you back? What is stopping you from doing what you want to do? What, if anything, can you do about it today?

CHOICES

59

Make no excuses when it comes to looking for a new job, as their presence will only stymie your success. Are you making any excuses now?

CHOICES

60

Change is a choice that comes with consequences. What, if anything, are you ready to change and make different choices about?

CHOICES

61

Know what you want and then figure out who can help you get it! Prevail until your goal is achieved … then, create a new one!

CHOICES

62

Focus on all the 'right' things about yourself instead of all the 'wrong' things. You will be happier and less stressed.

CHOICES

63

Do not be disappointed or disheartened by the people who will not help you; be immensely grateful to those who do.

CHOICES

64

Make a list of 10 things you love about yourself and 10 things you don't like about yourself? What, if anything, needs some refinement?

Motivation

MOTIVATION

65

As you embark upon the job hunt, purposely take a step back to assess assets, liabilities and your return-on-investment (ROI) to employer.

66

Launch your job search from a position of mental strength; let go of any baggage that will impede your full commitment to the job hunt.

MOTIVATION

67

Your work search will take longer than you think, be harder than expected and require a bigger investment of yourself than ever imagined.

MOTIVATION

68

Remind yourself daily of job search variables fully within your control: acceptance, actions, ambition, appearance, and attitude.

MOTIVATION

69

Look back with much confidence, no regret. Then, with one foot ahead of the other, deliberately and surely, find a way to carry on.

70

Career transition is a process of getting from point A to point B with high expectations, efficiency, excellence and, as fast as you can.

Personal Responsibility

PERSONAL RESPONSIBILITY

71

Take personal responsibility for your success. No one will do it for you. Adopt the motto, "If it's to be, it's up to me."

PERSONAL RESPONSIBILITY

72

Set and achieve S.M.A.R.T. goals.
S.M.A.R.T. goals are Specific, Measurable,
Achievable, Relevant and Time Bound.

PERSONAL RESPONSIBILITY

73

Spend your valuable time on only the things that will help you achieve your goals.

PERSONAL RESPONSIBILITY

74

Plan how you will achieve your goals. Then do whatever you have to do to achieve them.

PERSONAL RESPONSIBILITY

75

Success is a journey, not a destination. When you accomplish one goal reach higher and set a new one.

PERSONAL RESPONSIBILITY

76

Stuff will happen as you build your job success. Choose to respond positively to the negative stuff that happens.

PERSONAL RESPONSIBILITY

77

Failures are the tuition you pay for success. If you have a setback, react positively and keep at it until you succeed in your new job.

PERSONAL RESPONSIBILITY

78

Create a vivid mental image of yourself as a success in your new job. The more vivid the image, the more likely you'll be to achieve that success.

PERSONAL RESPONSIBILITY

79

Your vivid mental image is a blueprint, a plan for success. You have to do the work to make it a reality.

PERSONAL RESPONSIBILITY

80

Visualize the euphoria of success in your new job, not the pain of failure.

PERSONAL RESPONSIBILITY

81

Vision without action is a daydream. No matter how big your plans and dreams, they'll never become a reality until you act on them.

PERSONAL RESPONSIBILITY

82

Clarify your personal values. Your values are your anchor. They are your guides to decision making in ambiguous situations.

Self Confidence

SELF CONFIDENCE

83

Choose optimism. It builds your confidence.

84

Everyone is afraid sometime. Self confident people face their fears and act. Look your fears in the eye and do something.

SELF CONFIDENCE

85

Four steps to defeating the fear that can sabotage your success: Identify it. Admit it. Accept it. Do something about it.

SELF CONFIDENCE

86

Procrastination is the physical manifestation of fear and is a confidence killer. Act — especially when you're afraid.

SELF CONFIDENCE

87

Surround yourself with positive people. Hold them close. They will give you energy and help you create the success you want and deserve.

SELF CONFIDENCE

88

Jettison the negative people in your life. They are energy black holes. They will suck you dry.

SELF CONFIDENCE

89

Find a mentor. Mentors are positive people who will help you find the lessons in your problems and failures and how to use them to move forward.

SELF CONFIDENCE

90

Identify the self confident people you know. Watch how they act and carry themselves. Watch what they do. Act like them.

SELF CONFIDENCE

91

Fake it till you make it. Appear to be self-confident and others will treat you as if you are. In turn, this will boost your confidence!

SELF CONFIDENCE

92

Stand or sit up straight. Don't slouch. Your mother was right. Good posture is important. It makes you look self confident.

SELF CONFIDENCE

93

Be enthusiastic about the success of others. Help all the people around you recognize that they are special and valuable.

SELF CONFIDENCE

94

Take stock of yourself. What are your strengths? What are your weaknesses? Emphasize your strengths.

Positive
Personal Impact

POSITIVE PERSONAL IMPACT

95

Build your personal brand. Do whatever it takes to ensure that your boss and coworkers will think of you in the way you want them to.

POSITIVE PERSONAL IMPACT

96

Your personal brand should be unique to you, but built on integrity. Integrity is doing the right thing even when no one's looking.

POSITIVE PERSONAL IMPACT

97

Be visible. Volunteer for tough jobs.
Brand yourself as a person who can and
does makes significant contributions.

98

"Business" is the first and most important word in "business casual". Dress like you're going to work, not a sporting event or club.

POSITIVE PERSONAL IMPACT

99

Observe successful people in your organization. What do they wear? Dress like them and you won't go wrong.

POSITIVE PERSONAL IMPACT

100

21st Century technology has created new etiquette rules. Learn and use them to appear polished when you're online.

POSITIVE PERSONAL IMPACT

101

Always act like a lady or gentleman. It's not old fashioned; it's smart business and leads to a successful life and career.

POSITIVE PERSONAL IMPACT

102

Keep your breath fresh. Brush after meals and coffee. Use the strips. Don't chew gum. Ever. It makes you look like a cow.

POSITIVE PERSONAL IMPACT

103

Say "thank you" often. You'll succeed in your job, build a strong personal brand and leave a legacy of being a nice person.

POSITIVE PERSONAL IMPACT

104

Be courteous. It costs you nothing, and it can mean everything to a coworker. It also helps in getting what you want.

Outstanding Performance

OUTSTANDING PERFORMANCE

105

Become a lifelong learner. The half-life of knowledge is rapidly diminishing. Staying in the same place is the same as going backwards.

OUTSTANDING PERFORMANCE

106

Master your technical discipline. Share what you know. Become the "go to" person in your discipline in your company.

OUTSTANDING PERFORMANCE

107

Stay up to date on your industry. Read industry publications. Know the hot topics for your company, competitors and industry.

OUTSTANDING PERFORMANCE

108

Break large projects into smaller chunks.
They are not so overwhelming that way.
Set mini milestones for yourself.

OUTSTANDING PERFORMANCE

109

Get organized. Sweat the small stuff. Success is in execution. Execution is in the details.

OUTSTANDING PERFORMANCE

110

Positive time management is an important habit. Habits are like muscles. The more you use them, the stronger they get.

OUTSTANDING PERFORMANCE

111

The better you feel, the better you'll perform. Live a healthy lifestyle. Eat well. Exercise regularly. Get regular checkups.

OUTSTANDING PERFORMANCE

112

Determine your peak energy times. Schedule "high brain" tasks then and "low brain" tasks at times when your energy is lowest.

OUTSTANDING PERFORMANCE

113

Good truly is the enemy of great. Don't settle for good performance. Put in the effort necessary to become a great performer.

OUTSTANDING PERFORMANCE

114

Don't worry about getting credit for doing the job. Worry about getting the job done well — accurately and on time.

OUTSTANDING PERFORMANCE

115

Get the job done with what you've got. Don't worry about what you don't have or would like to have.

OUTSTANDING PERFORMANCE

116

Care about what you do. If you care a little, you'll be an OK performer. If you care a lot, you'll become a great performer.

Dynamic Communication

DYNAMIC COMMUNICATION

117

All dynamic communicators have mastered three basic communication skills: conversation, writing and presenting.

DYNAMIC COMMUNICATION

118

We're all in sales. You have to sell yourself every day. Become an excellent communicator to sell your ideas.

DYNAMIC COMMUNICATION

119

Learn how to handle yourself in conversation. A brief conversation with the right person can greatly help — or hinder your career.

DYNAMIC COMMUNICATION

120

Conversation tips: be warm, pleasant, gracious, and sensitive to the interpersonal needs and anxieties of others.

DYNAMIC COMMUNICATION

121

Listen more than you speak. Pay attention to what other people say; respond appropriately. Remember and use people's names.

DYNAMIC COMMUNICATION

122

Become a clear, concise writer. Make your writing easy to read and easy to understand. Use simple straightforward language.

DYNAMIC COMMUNICATION

123

Write clearly and simply: short words and sentences; first person; active voice. Be precise in your choice of words.

DYNAMIC COMMUNICATION

124

Presentation steps: 1. Determine the message. 2. Analyze the audience. 3. Organize the information. 4. Design visuals. 5. Practice.

DYNAMIC COMMUNICATION

125

Presentations are easy to create. Write your closing first, your opening next. Then fill in the content. Practice, practice, practice.

DYNAMIC COMMUNICATION

126

Practice presentations. You can control your nerves by practicing — out loud. The more you practice, the less afraid you'll be.

Relationship Building

RELATIONSHIP BUILDING

127

Get to know yourself. Use your self knowledge to better understand others and build relationships with them.

RELATIONSHIP BUILDING

128

When someone compliments you, say "thank you." When someone criticizes you, say "thank you, I'll work on that".

RELATIONSHIP BUILDING

129

Get genuinely interested in others. Bring out the best in everyone you know. Your colleagues and coworkers will gravitate to you.

RELATIONSHIP BUILDING

130

Keep confidences and avoid gossip. Don't embarrass others by repeating what they share with you — even if it isn't in confidence.

RELATIONSHIP BUILDING

131

Pay it forward. Build relationships with colleagues and coworkers by helping them with no expectation of return.

RELATIONSHIP BUILDING

132

When meeting a new coworker, ask yourself, "What can I do to help this person?" You'll build strong work relationships this way.

RELATIONSHIP BUILDING

133

There is no quid pro quo in effective work relationships. Do for others without being asked or waiting for them to do for you.

RELATIONSHIP BUILDING

134

Trust is the glue that holds relationships together. The more you demonstrate trust in others, the more they will trust you.

RELATIONSHIP BUILDING

135

Treat conflict as an opportunity to strengthen, not destroy, the relationships you've worked hard to build.

RELATIONSHIP BUILDING

136

Be a consensus builder. Focus on where you agree with other people. It will be easier to resolve differences and create agreement.

RELATIONSHIP BUILDING

137

Be responsible for yourself. No one can "make you angry". Choose to act in a civil, forthright, constructive manner in tense situations.

RELATIONSHIP BUILDING

138

Do your job; give credit to others for doing theirs. Everyone likes to work with people who share the credit for a job well done.

RELATIONSHIP BUILDING

139

We all make mistakes. Own up to yours. You'll become known as a straight shooter — honest with yourself and with others.

RELATIONSHIP BUILDING

140

Become widely trusted. Deliver on what you say you'll do. If you can't meet a commitment, let the other person know right away.

BONUS TWEET

141

Knowing is not enough. Successful people will read the advice in these tweets. And they will act on it. Be a successful person.

About Billie and Bud

@billiesucher ---> career transition expert invested in your #career #success. Let me know how I can help you: www.billiesucher.com.

@BudBilanich ---> life and career success coach helping you create the success you deserve. Let me help you succeed: www.BudBilanich.com

Success Tweets for Finding a Job and Excelling in It
makes a great gift!

Quantity discounts are available
from the publisher.

Call 303.393.0446 to inquire
about quantity pricing.

www.ingramcontent.com/pod-product-compliance
Lightning Source LLC
Chambersburg PA
CBHW060553200326
41521CB00007B/563